Just to say... Th

To:

Philemon 1:4
I always thank my God as I remember you in my prayers.
(New International Version)

From:

Hem your blessings with thankfulness
so they don't unravel.
Anon

Thank you for your friendship

Some people go to priests;
others to poetry;
I to my friends.

Virginia Woolf
English author, 1882–1941

From quiet homes and first beginning
Out to the undiscovered ends,
There's nothing worth the wear of winning,
But laughter and the love of friends.

Hilaire Belloc
Anglo-French author, 1870–1953

•

A man, sir, should keep his friendship in constant repair.

Samuel Johnson
English writer, 1709–1784

•

Friends are those rare people who ask how you are
and then wait for the answer.

Anon

Only your real friends will tell you
when your face is dirty.
Sicilian Proverb

Your friendship is so important to me!

Thank You

Friendship is the hardest thing in the
world to explain.
It's not something you learn in school.
But if you haven't learned the meaning
of friendship,
you really haven't learned anything.

Muhammad Ali
American boxer, 1942–present day

•

A friend is one that knows you as you
are, understands where you have been,
accepts what you have become, and
still, gently allows you to grow.

William Shakespeare
English poet and playwright, 1564–1616

•

Friends are part of the glue that holds
life and faith together. Powerful stuff.

Jon Katz
*American author and journalist,
1947– present day*

For each new morning with its light,
For rest and shelter of the night,
For health and food, for love
and friends,
For everything Thy goodness sends.

Ralph Waldo Emerson
American poet, 1803–1882

For these and so much more,
thank you, Lord.

Give thanks!

Thou that hast given so much to me,
give me one thing more, a grateful hear[t],
not thankful when it pleaseth me,
as if Thy blessings had spare days,
but such a heart whose pulse
may be Thy praise.

George Herbert
British poet, 1593–1633

Tony Thurlow, Iris

Lord, I'm grateful that I, too, have a place in your design.
Eddie Askew
Christian writer and former International Director
of The Leprosy Mission, 1927–2007

Abby Stonehall, Sparrow

I feel a very unusual sensation – if it is not indigestion,
I think it must be gratitude.
Benjamin Disraeli
British Prime Minister and statesman, 1804–1881

•

Silent gratitude isn't much use to anyone.
G.B. Stern
British novelist, 1890–1973

Thank you, Thank you, Thank you!

Thank you for your help

What do we live for, if not to make life less
difficult for each other?

George Eliot
English novelist, 1819–1880

You make my world a better place to be.

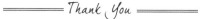

How wonderful it is that nobody need wait a single moment before starting to improve the world.
Anne Frank
Jewish Holocaust victim and diarist, 1929–1945

•

We can do no great things, only small things with great love.
Mother Teresa
Albanian Catholic nun, 1910–1997

•

Always set a high value on spontaneous kindness.
Samuel Johnson
English writer, 1709–1784

Nobody made a greater mistake than he who did nothing
because he could only do a little.
Edmund Burke
Irish statesman, 1729–1797

•

Wherever a man turns he can find someone who needs him.
Albert Schweitzer
German-French theologian, 1875–1965

•

I wondered why somebody didn't do something.
Then I realised, I am somebody.
Anon

•

The first question which the priest and the Levite asked was:
"If I stop to help this man, what will happen to me?"
But... The Good Samaritan reversed the question:
"If I do not stop to help this man, what will happen to him?"
Martin Luther King, Jr.
American clergyman, activist and leader, 1929–1968

Charity sees the need,
not the cause.
German Proverb

We make a living by what we get,

but we make a life by what we give.

Winston Churchill
British Prime Minister and statesman, 1874–1965

·

Ruth 2:12
May the LORD repay you for what you have done.
May you be richly rewarded by the LORD,
the God of Israel…

(New International Version)

Sheila Adams, Avenue of Autumn Trees

Give thanks again!

Gratitude is the best attitude.
Anon

•

It ought to be as habitual to us to thank as to ask.
C.H. Spurgeon
British Baptist preacher, 1834–1892

•

When you rise in the morning, give thanks for the light, for your life,
for your strength. Give thanks for your food and for the joy of living.
If you see no reason to give thanks, the fault lies in yourself.

Tecumseh
Native American leader, 1768–1813

══════ *Thank You* ══════

Who does not thank for little will not thank for much.
Estonian Proverb

•

When eating bamboo sprouts, remember the man who planted them.
Chinese Proverb

•

Most human beings have an almost infinite capacity for
taking things for granted.
Aldous Huxley
English novelist, 1894–1963

I really do appreciate all you do for me.

Ray Price, Daisies

Thank you for your kindness

At times our own light goes out and is rekindled by a spark from another person. Each of us has cause to think with deep gratitude of those who have lighted the flame within us.

Albert Schweitzer
German-French theologian, 1875–1965

Kindness is the language which the deaf can hear
and the blind can see.

Mark Twain
American writer, 1835–1910

•

Kindness is in our power, even when fondness is not.

Samuel Johnson
English writer, 1709–1784

•

Good words are worth much and cost little.

George Herbert
British poet, 1593–1633

Angela Allum, Clare College Gate

One act of thanksgiving when things go wrong with us is worth a thousand thanks when things are agreeable to our inclination.

John of Ávila
Spanish mystic, 1500–1569

·

The smallest act of kindness is worth more than the grandest intention.

Oscar Wilde
Irish playwright and poet, 1854–1900

·

Kindness, like a boomerang, always returns.

Anon

May all your kind acts return to you one hundred fold.

That best portion of a good man's life,
His little, nameless, unremembered acts
Of kindness and of love.

William Wordsworth
English poet, 1770–1850

Those who bring sunshine into the lives of others cannot keep it from themselves.

J.M. Barrie
Scottish author and dramatist, 1860–1937

Thank you for listening

The most precious gift we can offer
anyone is our attention.

Thich Nhat Hanh
Vietnamese Writer, 1926–present day

Thanks for your time – it means
so much to me.

James Norton, Giraffe

My wife says I never listen to her.
At least I think that's what she said.
Anon

We have two ears and one mouth so that
we can listen twice as much as we speak.

Epictetus
Greek philosopher, 55–135

•

Listen or thy tongue will keep thee deaf.

Native American Indian Proverb

•

Isn't it interesting that 'silent' and 'listen' are
spelled with the same letters?

Anon

Too often we underestimate the power of a touch,
a smile, a kind word, a listening ear, an honest compliment,
or the smallest act of caring, all of which have the
potential to turn a life around.

Leo Buscaglia
American author, 1924–1998

Give thanks always!

1 Thessalonians 5:16
Rejoice always, pray continually, give thanks in
all circumstances;
for this is God's will for you in Christ Jesus.
(New International Version)

All our discontents about what we want appeared to me to spring from the want of thankfulness for what we have.

Daniel Defoe
English writer and journalist, 1660–1731

I give it as my testimony that there is a marvellous
therapy in thanksgiving.

John Blanchard
British writer, 1932–present

•

God gave you a gift of 86,400 seconds today. Have you used one to say "thank you?"

William A. Ward
American writer, 1921–1994

Let me take a moment to say a great big THANK YOU!

Thank you for
just being you!

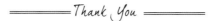
But if the while I think on thee, dear friend,
All losses are restored and sorrows end.
William Shakespeare
English poet and playwright, 1564–1616

•

In ordinary life we hardly realise that we receive a great
deal more than we give, and it is only with gratitude that
life becomes rich.
Dietrich Bonhoeffer
German Lutheran pastor, 1906–1945

Philemon 1:4
I always thank my God as I remember you in my prayers.
(New International Version)

•

Some people are so much sunshine to the square inch.

Walt Whitman
American poet 1819–1892

•

I would thank you from the bottom of my heart,
but for you my heart has no bottom.

Anon

If you're alone, I'll be your shadow.
If you want to cry, I'll be your shoulder.
If you want a hug, I'll be your pillow.
If you need to be happy, I'll be your smile.
But anytime you need a friend,
I'll just be me.

Anon

Psalm 100:4
Enter his gates with thanksgiving and his courts with praise;
give thanks to him and praise his name.
(New International Version)

•

Psalm 107:1
Give thanks to the LORD, for he is good;
his love endures for ever.
(New International Version)

•

Lord, dismiss us with Thy blessing,
Thanks for mercies past received.

John Sheffield
1st Duke of Buckingham and English poet,
1648–1721